THE
REALITY-BA$ED INVESTOR

THE
REALITY-BA$ED
INVESTOR

HOW TO ACHIEVE YOUR DREAM OF TOMORROW
STARTING FROM WHERE YOU ARE TODAY

JAY R. SPECTOR, CFP®

THE REALITY-BASED INVESTOR™
How to Achieve Your Dream of Tomorrow Starting from Where You Are Today

ISBN: 978-1-964046-98-3 (Paperback)
           978-1-964046-99-0 (Kindle)
           979-8-90343-000-0 (Hardcover)

Editing by Caroline Banton
Copyediting by Hannah Skaggs
Proofreading by Abby Larson
Illustrations by Norman Pitts
Text design and composition by Emily Fritz
Cover design by Casey Fritz

This book is dedicated to my wife, Bethany, and to my children, Jordyn and Micah, whose love, patience, and constant encouragement made this work possible. Your continued support through long days, difficult decisions, and countless hours of focus has been my foundation. You remind me daily why the work I do matters and what success truly means.

To my parents, Linda Spector and the late Mark Spector, thank you for the values, work ethic, and perspective you instilled in me. Your influence has shaped not only who I am, but how I approach both life and business. To my in-laws, Ellen and Bill Bresnick, thank you for your unwavering support, encouragement, and the role you've played in both my personal and professional journey.

To my EverVest financial team and my business partner, Elizabeth Mahoney, thank you for your collaboration, trust, and shared commitment to doing things the right way. Our aligned values, thoughtful conversations, and mutual respect continue to strengthen both our work and the impact we strive to have on others. To Kevin, Sid, Teresa, Andrea, Caleb, and Norm—thank you for your dedication to our clients and to our mission.

To my retired business partner, Sharon Barton, whose mentorship, leadership, and example established the foundation upon which this business—and this book—were built. Your guidance, integrity, and long-term perspective continue to influence my work well beyond the years we worked together.

And to my clients, past, present, and future, thank you for the trust you have placed in me to help you navigate your financial journey. It is an honor and a privilege to work with you and your families.

—JRS

CONTENTS

FOREWORD   1

PREFACE   3

PART I: INCOME FIRST, GROWTH SECOND   5
    The Reality of Retirement   7
    Why Retirement Is Different Today   8
    Making Your Own Paycheck   12

PART II: LIVING OFF, NOT ON, YOUR
INVESTMENTS   17
    What Is Reality-Based Planning?   19
    The Total Return Equation   24
    Planning Around Your Retirement Goals   25
    What Most People Get Wrong About
    Retirement   29

PART III: GAINING CLARITY: YOUR ZEN
GARDEN OF RETIREMENT PLANNING   33
    The Hidden Risks of Living Long and
    Spending Fast   35
    Social Security, Pensions, and What They
    Won't Cover   39
    Creating Streams of Income for Retirement   44

PART IV: HOW TO CREATE YOUR OWN
PAYCHECK IN RETIREMENT   49
    What's Your Income Gap?   51
    Income Strategies That Work   53
    High-Quality Investing—Creating
    Predictable Income with Lower Risk   60
    Tax-Smart Withdrawal Strategies   63
    Two Bites of the Apple   68

PART V: GROWTH IS INEVITABLE;
PROGRESS IS OPTIONAL   71
    Cutting Through the News and Noise   76
    Retirement Is Not the End—It's a New
    Beginning   85
    The Reality of Retirement   87

PART VI: WHO IS THE RIGHT FINANCIAL
ADVISOR FOR YOU?   89
    What You Should Expect from Your
    Financial Planner   91
    Questions to Ask Before You Hire a
    Financial Advisor   96
    Getting Real, Getting Started   98

ABOUT THE AUTHOR   101

FOREWORD

I have worked on Wall Street for over three decades and have had the great pleasure of working with Jay Spector and his former business partner, Sharon Barton, for nearly one of those decades. I always respected their level of professionalism, commitment to their clients, and business acumen. After reading *The Reality-Based Investor*, I now understand some of the ingredients that have made their business recipe so successful.

As Jay appropriately points out in this book, the role of a financial advisor when working with individual investors at or near retirement is, *"to allow them to retire feeling confident that they can live the lifestyle they want and that they've worked hard for."* The question then becomes how best to achieve this goal consistently. In an easy-to-read and easy-to-understand format, Jay walks through the basics of his Reality-Based Investing approach, including the important distinction between growth and income in the total return equation. Many individuals in retirement need sources of income to replace the income that they were previously receiving when employed. These same individuals are often concerned that they will run out of money at some point during their retirement and lose sleep at night as a result. A goal of reality-based retirement planning is to "*live off your investments, not on your investments*" according to Jay, for which I agree.

Grab a pen or highlighter and read *The Reality-Based Investor* if you want to learn how to put an investment plan in place to feel more comfortable about your retirement or understand different aspects of investing and financial planning in general.

—KEVIN MAHN, President and Chief Investment Officer of Hennion & Walsh Asset Management / SmartTrust® UITs

PREFACE

Retirement planning today is more complicated than ever. You're told to chase the market and time your withdrawals perfectly. You expect your retirement planning to work out across an unknowable future. But here's the truth: Retirement success doesn't come from perfection. It comes from preparation.

I've worked with hundreds of individuals and couples seeking a successful retirement. Some arrive with spreadsheets and binders, others with a few statements and a lot of questions, and some with nothing at all. Yet all of them have one thing in common: They're seeking clarity about their financial future.

That's why I wrote this book.

Reality-Based Investing™ is my framework. I believe it gives my clients more than just a projection. It strives to give them a plan they can understand and live with. The goal is to allow them to retire feeling confident that they can live the lifestyle they want and that they've worked hard for.

This book is about making retirement work in the real world: with real expenses, real fears, and real goals—and real income. It's about understanding how to use your money wisely. This book explains strategies designed to help generate a reliable paycheck. It will show you how to maintain control even when the market or life takes a turn.

There are no silver bullets here, no one-size-fits-all tactics. Just real strategies for real people. Reality-Based Investing is a flexible strategy that balances income, risk, and taxes.

This book is a down-to-earth guide to building a confident retirement plan, one that adapts with you. Read this book, and I believe it will be a resource you will return to again and again.

Ready to get started?

PART I

INCOME FIRST, GROWTH SECOND

The goal of retirement planning is simple: create an income stream that lasts as long as you do.

—Moshe Milevsky, author and professor of finance at York University

THE REALITY OF RETIREMENT

Retirement today looks much different than it did fifty or sixty years ago. If you retired back then, it was the era of the pension. Typically you worked for twenty to thirty years, and at the end of it, you were sent on your way with a gold watch and a certificate of appreciation. You picked up your briefcase, put on your fedora, and walked calmly off into the sunset.

In other words, you were looked after financially. You earned a salary while you were working and a pension once you stopped.

Unfortunately, the world has changed and that's just not the case anymore. The reality of retirement today is that few people have a pension plan or a defined-benefit plan. And I'll explain why in a moment.

What is a pension? A pension is a fixed payment that you receive each month. Social Security is, in effect, a pension payment. At least for now, retirees receive that payment for the rest of their lives.

Decades ago, pension payments were calculated based on how much a person earned and how many years they worked. People lived off their pensions in retirement. If they had savings, that money was in addition to their pension and their Social Security. Incredibly, many people could live comfortably on these two payments.

Today, pensions have largely disappeared. They have been replaced by defined-contribution plans, such as the good old 401(k) that we all know and love. The surprise has been the speed at which this occurred.

WHY RETIREMENT IS DIFFERENT TODAY

In 2020, only 3 percent of private-sector workers had access to a traditional pension. That year, 67 percent of them had access to some form of employer-provided retirement plan. However, the majority (52 percent) had access only to defined-contribution plans. And only 12 percent had access to both defined-benefit and defined-contribution plans.[1]

In 1980, retirement looked much different: 60 percent of private-sector workers had a pension. Within

---

1   "67 percent of private industry workers had access to retirement plans in 2020," The Economics Daily, March 1, 2021, Bureau of Labor Statistics, US Department of Labor, https://www.bls.gov/opub/ted/2021/67-percent-of-private-industry-workers-had-access-to-retirement-plans-in-2020.htm. Accessed August 20, 2025.

FAST FACTS

- Of private sector workers, 40 percent had a traditional pension in 1980.

- The number of private-sector workers with a traditional pension dropped 25 percent from 1980 to 2020.

- Of private-sector workers, only 3 percent had a traditional pension in 2020.

40 years, that number dropped from 60 percent to 3 percent. The drop could not have been steeper.

Fast Facts

- Of private sector workers, 40 percent had a traditional pension in 1980.

- The number of private-sector workers with a traditional pension dropped 25 percent from 1980 to 2020.

- Of private-sector workers, only 3 percent had a traditional pension in 2020.

Why did this happen?

Pension plans have largely disappeared because they're costly for employers. Managing a pension plan comes with huge administrative costs. Companies must adhere to rigorous compliance guidelines. Pension plans must also hit certain targets. They rely on market returns, which are unpredictable in volatile markets.

Increasing lifespans are also playing a role. If a company employee retires at age sixty-five and lives to age ninety-five, they receive that pension for the rest of their life. That's an increasingly heavy financial burden for the company that employs them. In the mid-1960s, average life expectancy was sixty-seven to seventy-four years.[2] Today, life expectancy is seventy-six to eighty-one years.

We have a higher cost of living today also. If you retired in the 1950s or 1960s, there was less to worry about financially. Your twilight years were supported by your pension and Social Security. Once you were gone, your family inherited your house and your personal items, and that was about it.

Pensions did come with risk for the employee. In the case of company bankruptcy, their pension either disappeared or was cut.

In 2005, United Airlines defaulted on $9 billion worth of pension obligations. It was the largest such default in US history. The Pension Benefit Guarantee Corporation (PBGC), which faced its own solvency crisis, took over the United pensions, but some pilots saw their pensions cut to less than half the previous amount.[3] Many employees struggled to pay medical costs and mortgages.

---

2   Table V.A3.—"Period Life Expectancies, Calendar Years 1940–2001," Social Security Administration, March 6, 2002, https://www.ssa.gov/OACT/TR/TR02/lr5A3-h.html.

3   Dale Russakoff, "Failing Pensions Exact a Human Toll," NBC News, June 12, 2005, https://www.nbcnews.com/id/wbna8196565.

The costs and financial risk encouraged employers to change their retirement plan policies. Instead of funding pension plans, they began offering defined-contribution plans like the 401(k), putting the onus on employees.

Defined-contribution plans are based on contributions from the employee, often with an employer match. This model transferred the investment risk to the employee, which appealed to employers.

The change gave rise to financial planners like me. When pensions were rife, the retirement planning industry was a shadow of what it is today. People didn't seek out ways to fund their retirement on a grand scale.

But that's all changed.

Today, retirement planning is a huge industry. Approximately 321,000 personal financial advisors are active in the United States.[4] People have realized that they don't just lose a paycheck when they retire; they have to make their own paycheck.

MAKING YOUR OWN PAYCHECK

The 401(k) emerged during the 1970s. In 1974, federal legislation created the Employee Retirement Income

---

4   US Bureau of Labor Statistics, "Personal Finance Advisors," in *Occupational Outlook Handbook*, US Department of Labor, April 18, 2025, https://www.bls.gov/ooh/business-and-financial/personal-financial-advisors.htm.

and Security Act (ERISA). The law brought more onerous requirements for pension funds.[5]

The requirements were problematic for business owners. As an alternative to costly pension funds, the 401(k) was officially launched in the early 1980s.[6] And once the new plan started to gain traction, pensions started to disappear.

It was a relatively easy transition. Defined-contribution plans gave employees more control of their retirement savings, and so the number of workers making defined contributions skyrocketed. Workers could choose the amount they contributed to their retirement savings, up to the limits of federal law.

What employees were not aware of was that the new plans placed more responsibility on them. They were now on the hook to make money out of those savings—enough money to sustain them when they retired. In other words, workers now had to create their own paycheck in retirement.

<hr>

5   Employee Benefits Security Administration, "History of EBSA and ERISA," US Department of Labor, accessed August 20, 2025, https://www.dol.gov/agencies/ebsa/about-ebsa/about-us/history-of-ebsa-and-erisa.

6   Kathleen Elkins, "A Brief History of the 401(k), Which Changed How Americans Retire," CNBC, January 4, 2017, https://www.cnbc.com/2017/01/04/a-brief-history-of-the-401k-which-changed-how-americans-retire.html.

The 401(k) is a portable plan, meaning you can take it with you when you leave an employer. The money you've contributed is yours, and its long-term outcome depends on how you've invested it. Poor investment choices can impact performance, but the plan itself remains intact and transferable.

From the employer's perspective, 401(k) plans are easier to administer and thus lower costs. Employees can visit their 401(k) website and select the funds in which they want to invest. They can also update and make changes to their contributions each year, up to a certain limit.

What is more challenging for people is turning that money into a steady income stream for when they retire. That's where a financial planner comes in. Our goal is to help you create that paycheck.

The retirement paycheck is generated from your assets. It will pay for your living costs plus unexpected expenses, such as current and future medical costs.

As I mentioned, average life expectancies are longer now, and people face steeper medical expenses later in life as their health deteriorates. This adds complexity to retirement planning. If you don't have resources set aside to cover those expenses, your nest egg will disappear quickly. That means you have to not only make a paycheck in retirement but also sustain it over hopefully a long time frame.

I advise people to get a handle on as many of their variable expenses as they can. How and where are you spending money? Once we have a clear picture of your incoming funds and outgoing expenses, we can start to plan. We can consider unforeseen expenses and cost-of-living increases. Most importantly, we can find ways to create streams of income.

PART II
LIVING OFF, NOT ON, YOUR INVESTMENTS

Don't work for money; make it work for you.

—Robert Kiyosaki

WHAT IS REALITY-BASED PLANNING?

The reality-based retirement planning philosophy is to live *off* your investments, not *on* your investments. Your investment accounts must produce the income you need in retirement. That's on a before-and-after-tax basis. End of story.

Some people follow the 4 percent distribution rule and consider it the path to a successful retirement. It's a popular philosophy, but I consider it unreliable. Investopedia defines the 4 percent rule as follows:

> The 4 percent rule is a retirement withdrawal guideline suggesting retirees withdraw 4 percent of their retirement account in the first year and adjust that amount for inflation annually. This strategy aims to sustain funds for approximately 30 years, relying on investment returns to

The reality-based retirement planning philosophy is to live off your investments, not on your investments. Your investment accounts must produce the income you need in retirement. That's on a before-and-after-tax basis.

provide a steady income stream from interest and dividends.[7]

Where this is flawed is that the rule does not consider when you start investing. It also does not factor in when you start taking distributions from your account. Sell shares at the wrong time, such as when the market is down, and you'll have to sell more shares to get the income you need.

For example, the stock market fell 777.68 points in intraday trading in March 2009. In just thirty-three days in early 2020, during the COVID-19 pandemic, the S&P 500 plunged 34 percent. Withdrawing retirement income at those times was costly. You would have had to sell more shares of your investments to generate 4 percent income because those shares were worth less.

Once you sell assets, they're no longer in your account and growing for you when the market recovers.

Past performance doesn't dictate future performance. You can look at the market movements over time and surmise that the 4 percent rule generally works. However, timing also counts. When you retire and how you generate income are factors to consider. Effective planning is not just about the assets you hold.

---

7   Julia Kagan, "What Is the 4 Percent Rule for Withdrawals in Retirement?," Investopedia, July 25, 2025, https://www.investopedia.com/terms/f/four-percent-rule.asp.

I'm referring to the sequencing of distribution and the sequencing of timing. These factors play into the Reality-Based Investing philosophy.

Let me be clear: We're not looking to sell shares of an investment to provide you with the monthly income you need. We're using the *income* from the investments (dividends[8] and interest) to provide you with the income you need. This is living *off* the investment, not *on* the investment.

Reality-based planning helps to ensure you have the resources available when you need them. Most people face unexpected expenses from time to time, like having to buy a new car or fix the air conditioning. The goal is to be in control of your investments so that you can sell a portion to generate the cash you need. Think of it as more of an on-demand model than a spend-as-you-go model.

Ideally, if you do face an emergency and have to sell capital, it will affect your income only slightly. The goal is to make sure there's growth in your investment plan to outpace inflation. We focus on long-term progress, not annual returns.

This is a key point. People like to talk about their annual returns. They like to think an 8 percent or 10

---

8 Dividend payments are not guaranteed and may be reduced or eliminated at any time by the issuing company.

percent return is worth talking about. Have you ever met someone at a party or a dinner who wants to talk to you about their return on investments? I call the number they throw out their "cocktail number."

"What are you getting from your guy?" they'll ask (they always assume it's a guy and never a woman). "Eight percent? Well, that's great. I got ten last year."

But when you hear that nonsense, ask yourself, *What is that number actually made up of? How did they calculate it?*

I ask that question because the equation for total return is dividends plus market growth. So, you have to understand the nexus of that equation—there are two components, not just market growth.

Next time you talk cocktail numbers with someone, ask them to be specific and break down the number for you. It might be enlightening for them.

THE TOTAL RETURN EQUATION

Reality-Based Investing relies on that total return equation. It espouses that you want to live off one half of it—your dividends. That way, your principal can still grow and provide more income. Living off dividends and interest is how people are successful in retirement.

You might hear at a college orientation, "Look to your left, and look to your right; one of those two people won't graduate." I challenge you to look to the family next door and the family down the street.

One family could be worrying about their retirement if they haven't saved enough. But there could also be a quiet millionaire who has been socking away money in a 401(k) account for the last twenty or thirty years.

These are the people who will be incredibly successful in retirement. They may even have more than they need to cover their monthly spending. That's why there's an RV parked in the driveway and they're taking trips to see the grandkids every month.

These people earn more in retirement than they earned working because they saved. They have the resources in their portfolio. They have Social Security to help them meet or exceed what they were generating while working.

I often meet with clients who want to retire and who have saved diligently and planned well. When I show them their numbers, they say, "Wow, this is great. I don't know why I don't retire today. I'm making more now than I did when I was working."

PLANNING AROUND YOUR RETIREMENT GOALS

Your needs and vision for retirement will be unique. That's why Reality-Based Investing is a philosophy-based planning strategy. It's not a cookie-cutter, one-size-fits-all approach.

The first step is to understand your needs and goals. From there, we can design an investment income plan tailored to you and your stage in life. And you can reinvest the income generated by your existing investments. You can do this in your thirties, forties, fifties, or sixties. Reinvestment means buying more shares, which can result in a higher total return over time. In short, we develop customized investment strategies.

How does Reality-Based Investing differ from other investing strategies? Some financial planners rely on algorithm-based financial planning software. They calculate what your situation might be in thousands of different market scenarios and show you how confident you can be in your ability to retire based on the inputs you plug in.

That sounds great. It gives people some level of comfort. But to me, it's not reality. Reality is not an algorithm leading to an algorithm-generated confidence level. Retiring is a huge life decision, and I believe you need more than that to have peace of mind that you can retire comfortably.

As well as a reality-based approach, there's another component to my investing framework. Reality-Based Investing is hard work. There's no getting away from the fact that it takes hard work to be successful in retirement.

With algorithm-based investing, you might commit to saving $50,000 for retirement every year. But life happens. And the minute you don't save what you committed to, you blow up your plan.

Years ago, we developed a comprehensive financial plan for a client that clearly demonstrated long-term success—provided one key commitment was honored. They had to save $50,000 per year as they said they would (and could). As part of the financial planning process, the client agreed that this annual contribution was essential to keeping the plan on track. However,

Reality-Based Investing

is hard work. There's no

getting away from the fact

that it takes hard work to be

successful in retirement.

after the first year ended, they never made the planned contribution. In the years that followed, not only did their annual savings fall short but their portfolio distributions consistently exceeded the income the portfolio generated.

This resulted in their investment principal being repeatedly tapped earlier and more aggressively than what we had planned. Over time, this erosion materially reduced the overall probability of success of their retirement income plan. The challenge wasn't market performance or investment strategy—it was the gap between the plan on paper and real-life behavior.

So, what's the answer? Don't use an algorithm. Don't come up with a random number you think you can save each year. Be honest with yourself as to what you can realistically save.

Reality-Based Investing says, "Okay, yes, you need to save money on an annual basis." Yes, you need to maximize your opportunities, but essentially, you're responsible for what you generate. You generate what you want from the investments you've put together. There are targets, and there are guides, but it's up to you to create what you need.

The sooner you get started on this, the better. You might have to commit to putting away more to fund your retirement if you're not in a great position financially.

For example, if you tell me you have $25,000 and are ready to retire, I'm going to ask you what your budget is. I'll probably say to you that you will want to keep working because you won't be able to meet your budget needs and have enough resources to live the retirement that you want and the lifestyle to which you're accustomed. You'll need to find a way to make ends meet. It could mean continuing to work well into your seventies and eighties. Social Security alone will not afford you the lifestyle you want in retirement.

Unfortunately, we do see people in this situation. They didn't save enough for retirement, and they have to work into their seventies and eighties. They don't have the luxury of stopping work. They don't have a nest egg that can generate tens of thousands of dollars. They have little income to supplement their Social Security.

Hard work is what it takes.

WHAT MOST PEOPLE GET WRONG ABOUT RETIREMENT

People underestimate their retirement needs. They're not thinking about their need to make a paycheck after they stop working. They rely on the 4 percent retirement distribution "rule," which isn't a rule at all. It's more of a gamble.

The 4 percent rule might work for some people, but there are other less risky paths to take. The beauty of Reality-Based Investing for retirement is that it doesn't rely on the markets. You won't be feeding the "fear-greed" index. You won't be turning to meditation to calm your nerves when the market takes a turn for the worse.

Creating a paycheck based on dividend income and interest payments can be a reliable strategy. Part of it is planning a withdrawal strategy that doesn't take a big bite out of your principal. Now, if companies start withholding dividends[9] or bonds go into default, we have a bigger problem. However, by and large, dividends and interest payments are reliable and consistent.

Volatility certainly affects the value of your portfolio. However, with a reality-based framework, your paycheck in retirement is based on the number of shares you own. It's not based on their value. Likewise, you're paid based on the number of bonds you own, not the value of those bonds. It's straightforward, and it's a time-tested formula. That's the framework within which we work. Market volatility is not a driving factor.

---

9   Dividend payments are not guaranteed and may be reduced or eliminated at any time by the issuing company.

I had one client who was deeply worried that she was going to run out of money even though her portfolio was designed to generate reliable dividend and interest income. She called the office several times a week to "check in," seeking reassurance that everything was still okay.

Ironically, while she lived off the income her portfolio produced, she consistently spent far less than what it generated each month. Her fear wasn't rooted in numbers or market performance; it was rooted in uncertainty. She was simply afraid that she would run out of money.

We reframed her plan around income received, not investment assets sold, and walked her through month after month to help her gain confidence that her income exceeded her needs.

PART III
GAINING CLARITY

Your Zen Garden of Retirement Planning

Dividends are the investor's tangible return on investment, the only return that cannot be faked.

—Geraldine Weiss, famed editor and writer

THE HIDDEN RISKS OF LIVING LONG AND SPENDING FAST

People are living longer, which is wonderful. But that means we all need more money in retirement, and a large reason for that is we may face unexpected medical expenses. *The Fidelity 2025 Annual Report* estimated that a sixty-five-year-old who retires in 2025 can expect to spend an average of $172,500 on healthcare and medical

We're living longer, spending

faster, and spending more.

To combat this phenomenon,

the principle of Reality-

Based Investing is to

create a balance in income

distribution so that you can

afford financial events like

unexpected healthcare costs.

expenses during their retirement. And these costs don't include long-term care.[10]

We're living longer, spending faster, and spending more.

To combat this phenomenon, the principle of Reality-Based Investing is to create a balance in income distribution so that you can afford financial events like unexpected healthcare costs. What exactly do I mean by "a balance of income distribution"? I mean making sure you're taking income generated by your investments, not your principal.

People often think, *I'm just going to take 5 percent of my portfolio every year*, and then they also take an extra $15,000, $20,000, or $100,000 here or there. That becomes a problem. They don't realize these extra distributions will impact their income and upend the balance significantly.

For example, way down the road, if you need to take principal distributions each year, perhaps for major purchases or medical issues, it would be ideal if you could do so at will. You don't want to find yourself

---

10   Fidelity Newsroom, "Fidelity Investments® Releases 2025 Retiree Health Care Cost Estimate, a Timely Reminder for All Generations to Begin Planning," press release, Fidelity Investments, July 30, 2025, https://newsroom.fidelity.com/pressreleases/fidelity-investments—releases-2025-retiree-health-care-cost-estimate—a-timely-reminder-for-all-gen/s/3c62e988-12e2-4dc8-afb4-f44b-06c6d52e.

in a situation where the market is dictating to you when and how you take distributions and how many shares you need to sell.

This ties into the sequencing of your distributions, which I talked about in the previous chapter. The market dictates to you if you're not in a balanced position. Let's say you need $100,000 to buy an RV, so you decide to sell shares. You might have to sell in a down market, which means you'll have to sell more shares to get that $100,000 than you would in a better market.

If you're always selling more shares than you previously needed to because of the market, that will blow up your income plan. Once your shares are gone, you have fewer assets to produce income for you.

So planning for your retirement is a matter of balancing what you need and the sources of income you have. If you need cash, consider whether you can tap other pensions or income sources instead of your principal. Do you have rental income or money squirreled away in the bank that you could use? We want to set up these alternatives so that the market is not a concern.

Be careful about keeping money in the bank. If you're retired and you have a pot of cash in a bank account, that cash is better off in an investment where it can make money for you—like a high-yield savings account or a certificate of deposit.

The point is that when you spend some of your liquid cash or your reserve, it's not making money for you anymore. Once it's spent, it's spent. Balance comes when you focus on preserving the assets you have because the future is unknown.

Part of that future is Social Security, at least for now. So, let's look at the role of Social Security. And let's also look at pensions, for those lucky enough to have one.

SOCIAL SECURITY, PENSIONS, AND WHAT THEY WON'T COVER

Social Security is a major topic of discussion in the media and among government officials. It's true that the government is currently borrowing against the Social Security trust fund to cover its bills.

According to the Social Security Administration, its benefits will be paid in full until 2037. After that, the trust fund reserves are projected to become exhausted. When that happens, the taxes collected should be sufficient to pay just 76 percent of benefits.

If Congress doesn't make changes and find additional revenue sources for the program, the Board of Trustees projects an immediate reduction in benefits of approximately 13 percent. Alternatively, the board claims there could be an increase in the combined payroll tax rate from 12.4 percent to 14.4 percent, or a combination of the two. If such an increase occurs, that would allow full payment of the scheduled benefits for the next seventy-five years.[11]

We don't know what the government is going to do with Social Security, but it's currently indicating a desire to get out of the business of social safety nets. So, I recommend planning as though Social Security won't be there when you retire. If you plan as though it will, you might find yourself a couple of thousand dollars in the hole every month when you do retire.

There are proposals to means-test payments based on your income. For example, if you have a certain amount of income, you might be phased out of Social Security. There are also proposals to privatize Social Security. If it were privatized, administrators of the funds might give you a pot of money based on what you've paid into the program, and you could invest it in the market.

Social Security was not meant to be the beginning and end of your retirement income. It was meant to supplement that income only. Back in the day, your Social Security plus your pension was your retirement. That model is not sustainable today.

11   Stephen C. Goss, "The Future Financial Status of the Social Security Program," *Social Security Bulletin* 70, no. 3 (2010): 111–126, https://www.ssa.gov/policy/docs/ssb/v70n3/v70n3p111.html.

Social Security was not meant to be the beginning and end of your retirement income. It was meant to supplement that income only. Back in the day, your Social Security plus your pension was your retirement. That model is not sustainable today.

The cost of living has gone through the roof exponentially. Pensions have gone away, and people now have to make their own paycheck. Congress, if left to their own devices, will change the rules of Social Security, and even though it's an entitlement to those of us who have worked hard and paid into it, it very well may not be there when we need it.

The bottom line: Social Security and pensions will go only so far.

Pensions are also petering out. Having a pension plan is wonderful, but only if you make wise choices regarding the plan. Pensions come with different payment options, and which one you choose will have a significant effect on your income in retirement. The two main types of pension are single life and joint life, but there's also an option called joint certain.

SINGLE LIFE PENSION OPTION

A single life payment option is for the pension holder only. If you're the holder, the payment is paid to you in perpetuity in retirement. Once you pass away, unfortunately, your benefits don't go to your spouse, and they'll have to make up the lost income from some other source.

JOINT LIFE PENSION OPTION

A joint life pension option is paid to two spouses and typically pays a death benefit once for either person's death. You can choose a "first-to-die" pension or a "second-to-die" pension. As the name implies, a first-to-die pension pays out a death benefit upon the death of the first spouse, and a second-to-die pension pays the benefit only after the second person on the policy dies. Joint life pensions are often useful for estate planning.

LIFE CERTAIN JOINT PENSION OPTION

A life certain joint pension guarantees monthly payments for a set period after one person dies or when certain conditions are met. These pensions provide a steady income to a participant for their lifetime, with some amount continuing for a guaranteed "certain" period to a surviving beneficiary after the participant's death.

If you are the pension holder, you'll receive a payment that is reduced to accommodate the payments to the beneficiary. The amount of the reduction might be 50 percent, 75 percent, or 100 percent of the planned payment to the survivor. The higher your age, the less you will receive initially as a payout.

Choosing the right pension option can secure your family's future and ensure the income doesn't go away when the pension holder dies. Remember, however, that pensions are not guaranteed. Your pension could be at risk if the providing company goes bankrupt.

As I mentioned before, in the United Airlines bankruptcy in 2005, there were 121,500 United workers participating in the company's pension plan.[12] When the company filed for bankruptcy, the pension plan went away. The United States government took over the plan, and pilots who had been used to earning around $200,000 a year then received only 20–25 percent of that amount. Losing $150,000 a year is hard for a family to make up for.

Because there are risks associated with so many income-producing vehicles, let's look at how best to structure your retirement plan with as many options for income as possible.

CREATING STREAMS OF INCOME FOR RETIREMENT

According to Vanguard, in 2023, more than 60 million Americans participated in 401(k) plans, and the average balance for someone aged fifty-five to sixty-four

---

12   James F. Peltz, "United Airlines Cleared to Shed Pension Plans," *Los Angeles Times*, May 11, 2005, https://www.latimes.com/archives/la-xpm-2005-may-11-fi-united11-story.html.

Nobody's going to take care of you in retirement. And that's why you need reliable streams of income: a pension or 401(k), Social Security, and annuities.

was $232,000. As mentioned, the 401(k) is now the primary retirement savings vehicle for most people in the United States, especially in the private sector.

A balance of $232,000 will not go very far. Let's say you spend $4,000 a month on your retirement expenses—housing, food, travel. You need $4,000 a month after taxes to meet your budget. If you have only $232,000, you're going to have a very difficult time trying to cover your expenses for more than about four years. And what about unexpected bills?

Nobody's going to take care of you in retirement. And that's why you need reliable streams of income: a pension or 401(k), Social Security, and annuities. I'll talk more about annuities later in the book.

First, let's just look quickly at how to structure your retirement planning. For that, I like to use what I call the "income pyramid."

THE INCOME PYRAMID

A pyramid is a strong, stable structure, and your portfolio should be just as enduring. The foundation of the pyramid is the most important part. As the illustration shows, your Social Security forms the first layer of your pyramid, and the second layer is your pension if you have one. These, at least for now, are the most reliable

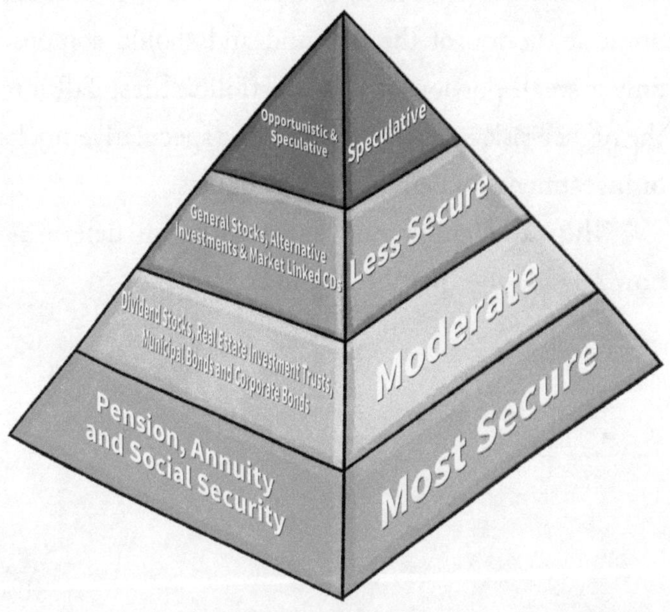

sources of income. The next layer is made up of annuities because they're also reliable.

Then, on top of that strong foundation, you need to have other streams of income from passive investments. These might be real estate and rental income, stocks, and qualified retirement accounts like individual retirement accounts (IRAs). A nonqualified plan is a tax-deferred, employer-sponsored retirement plan that does not meet Employee Retirement Income Security Act (ERISA) standards. These investments are less reliable than a pension or Social Security, but they're still relatively safe.

Your most unreliable sources of income form the point at the top of the pyramid and should compose only a small portion of your portfolio. These fall into the higher-risk category—things like speculative stocks or investments in early-stage companies.

The way your pyramid is structured will determine how reliable your paycheck is in retirement.

PART IV
HOW TO CREATE YOUR OWN PAYCHECK IN RETIREMENT

Security comes not from the assets themselves but from the income they produce.

—Anonymous

WHAT'S YOUR INCOME GAP?

I mentioned the need for balance in the last chapter. Balance applies in many aspects of retirement planning. For example, a balanced budget is one that allows you to pay all your expenses and monthly bills and have some left over to save. A balanced portfolio is one that is diversified and reflects a level of risk that's appropriate for you.

If your income is less than your expenses, you don't have balance; you have an income gap. And that gap needs to be closed before you can start to build a balanced portfolio and thus a balanced retirement plan.

Getting a handle on your monthly expenses is job number one. To do that, find out what you're spending on a monthly or annual basis. See if you can chip away at some of those expenses and achieve a net zero or a net positive on the income side.

Tip: Track every dollar you earn and spend in a month to get a sense of your recurring, essential, and discretionary spending.

Next, look at your sources of income—Social Security, pension, annuity, whatever constitutes the

If your income is less than your expenses, you don't have balance; you have an income gap. And that gap needs to be closed before you can start to build a balanced portfolio and thus a balanced retirement plan.

foundation of your pyramid. Look further up your pyramid. See if the income you might have from dividends or interest can make up the gap.

If you can't make up the gap using additional income sources or the investments you've saved, then it's time to have a hard conversation with yourself. You're going to have to cut expenses significantly, which will require making sacrifices.

If you want to retire early and enjoy the fruits of your labor when you do, you have to make sure your debits equal or are less than your credits. And if you can't do that, something has to give. That is, you have to find a way to get more income in versus more money going out.

INCOME STRATEGIES THAT WORK

As I said before, many advisors use sophisticated software to help them generate retirement plans. Those plans come with a confidence measure, which is basically the probability that you'll ultimately reach your financial goals. But the problem I see with this type of modeling is that the calculations assume you'll adhere to all the variables that were plugged into the software in the first place.

For example, will you successfully put away $500 a month with no exceptions? What happens in a financial emergency? If you lose your job or need medical care, will you still save that amount or will you have to dig into your investment account? What if Social Security is not there? What if the company that holds your pension goes bankrupt?

However, I don't find that sophisticated models generated by artificial intelligence (AI) are a realistic approach. I prefer an income-generation approach—a plan and a model that requires you to generate income from your assets.

Income is generated by the assets you hold. This is reality, not a simulation. It's saying, "Here's what you have in your portfolio, and here's what you can get out of it based on your risk tolerance and your investment time horizon"—your age, in other words. This approach is a way to make your money work for you now so that you have income later.

Here's an example of what I'm talking about: Let's say you have $1 million to invest. Through dividends and interest, it can conservatively generate $50,000 a year. That's a 5 percent dividend income yield.

Let's also say you need $7,000 a month ($84,000 a year) to live on after tax, and you have $100,000 available in earnings. No problem. You have $100,000 available in income. You're fine. You don't have to sell any investments.

However, let's look at a scenario in which you're generating $50,000 pretax each year, and you're in a 20 percent tax bracket. In this case, you have $40,000 of income after paying tax. Let's say your expenses are $4,000 a month, which adds up to $48,000 a year that you need to live.

In this scenario, your $40,000 in income won't be enough after tax to meet your budget. You have an income gap of $8,000 that needs to be closed. That will mean either reducing your expenses or finding additional income to bridge the gap.

If you don't fill that income gap, you can't generate more income. Reality-Based Investing is simple. It's generating income from your savings, and it all starts with your budget. Get that right, and everything else follows.

Contrary to popular opinion, there's no magic number that says you have to have X number of dollars to retire. That's because that approach doesn't take into account what you're spending in retirement or your other investments or income sources.

UNDERSTANDING YOUR COCKTAIL NUMBER (TOTAL RETURN)

Assets are invested with growth in mind. Growth is important, but it's not the focus of a reality-based

Reality-Based Investing is simple. It's generating income from your savings, and it all starts with your budget. Get that right, and everything else follows.

approach to retirement. Why? Because growth is not reliable. It's nice to have, but only income is reliable.

We're currently in the midst of a market driven by a technology-fueled craze. For years, the five FAAMG stocks—Meta (formerly Facebook), Apple, Amazon, Microsoft, and Alphabet's Google have dominated the news. Now, artificial intelligence has taken the lead and dominates the news. If you invested in the technology sector, you have more money in your portfolio than when you started. That's fantastic. Congratulations! However, the current state of the market will change. Some of those growth stocks will falter. The market could crash.

That's why the goal of retirement and financial planning is to create reliable and consistent income. There might be years when the market is down 10–15 percent, but if you've created an income stream from your investments, that income will remain reliable and consistent. The market value pullback won't have an effect on your day-to-day spending. Or at least it will have an effect only when you need to sell a portion of your principal.

What I'm describing is total return. It's not the same as the average annual return on a few stocks. Your total return is how much income you're generating from your retirement pyramid structure, not the average return you're getting from your Charles Schwab or Fidelity account.

A LOOK AT REAL TOTAL RETURN

Total return is a math equation:

GROWTH + INCOME = TOTAL RETURN

If you're relying on growth, which, remember, is unreliable, then your total return on a portfolio is the income you're generating. Conversely, if you have no income and you're relying on growth, your total return is just the growth. We seek some harmony between growth and income to get a strong total return.

Younger investors, those in their twenties, thirties, and forties, can afford to take an aggressive approach to total return investing because they have a longer time horizon. They can take more risk. They can reinvest their dividends and buy more shares every month to yield a greater total return over time.

Older investors, those in their late fifties to eighties, have to be more conservative because they're relying on their portfolio. They're also looking for a total return, but they will be using one half of the equation for their retirement income and leaving the other half in place to grow their portfolio and hopefully outpace inflation.

Have I confused you? The main point to remember is that the total return equation means something different for every investor. Total return is a critical number for me as a financial advisor, a number I need to determine when helping clients. But I also want you to understand that total return is just a math equation. It's made up of two components: growth and income. It's not an arbitrary figure based on the markets.

Let me explain this concept another way. Retiree investors rely on their portfolio to produce the monthly income they got from their paychecks while working. As an example, suppose you, as a retiree, receive dividends from stock you hold, and you reinvest those dividends. In this case, you're using the stock to produce lost income, and that replacement income is the dividend payouts you receive, not stock that you sell.

When younger investors have time on their side, they can let those dividends and interest payments compound and buy more shares. Then, next month, they have more shares that produce more dividends that they can reinvest and benefit once again from the compound effect.

The result? Their portfolio grows over time, and their income increases over time. This is what we call high-quality investing. It produces growth and income.

This is the cocktail number you *should* be talking about.[13]

HIGH-QUALITY INVESTING—CREATING PREDICTABLE INCOME WITH LOWER RISK

If we look at the income pyramid again, the base layer is composed of your pension and Social Security. Above that layer are assets that will add additional juice to your portfolio. These assets have to be worth the

13 Dividend payments are not guaranteed and may be reduced or eliminated at any time by the issuing company.

squeeze, however. That means they have to be worth the level of risk you're exposing them to.

You have to make sure that whatever you're doing to generate more juice in your portfolio is appropriate for your risk level. Your risk level depends on many factors, such as your age and your current financial standing.

When we look for other assets to add to this layer, we're also looking for ways to generate interest and dividend income. Popular vehicles for this are tax-free municipal bonds, corporate bonds, and dividends generated by common stock.

As I discussed earlier, interest and dividend income can be considered "reliable income." Annuities are another form of income—albeit guaranteed income—because they're guaranteed by the underlying insurance company.[14]

Annuities get a bad rap. There are so many TV commercials for them that people think they're a con. People say annuities are bad or annuities are expensive. They can be expensive, but you have to know what you're buying and why. Before you buy an investment, know the purpose of that investment and the cost.

The annuity industry has been turned upside down in recent decades. There are now lower-cost annuity

---

14 Guarantees are based on the claims paying ability of the issuing company.

investments that provide income insurance for clients. These investments can be perfect for that second layer of your income pyramid.

Certain annuities are appropriate for certain circumstances. They're not a one-size-fits-all approach for everybody. However, they can fit the bill if you're looking to guarantee a minimum portion of your retirement income. There are dozens of annuity options; just make sure that whatever you look at is appropriate for your given situation.

Another aspect of creating your own paycheck in retirement is structuring withdrawals from your various retirement and asset accounts. When you start to draw funds from your various accounts, there are significant tax implications that can drastically affect your income.

TAX-SMART WITHDRAWAL STRATEGIES

I like to call the draw-down process the "sequencing of distributions." It's quite methodical, and there is a method to it.

SEQUENCING OF DISTRIBUTIONS

Theoretically, it sounds like you would want to draw down your lowest-taxed investment dollars first. You generally take from your taxable account first, then from tax-deferred accounts (think IRAs), while letting the Roth IRA (tax-free) grow last.

However, there are situations when taking from your traditional IRA first—and letting the Roth IRA continue growing—makes the most sense. The right choice, meaning the right account, depends on your personal tax situation.

Because traditional IRA withdrawals are taxable and Roth IRA withdrawals are tax-free, most people prefer to use traditional IRA funds first. That preserves the Roth IRA for later years or to pass on to children or grandchildren. Recent tax laws passed by Congress make the Roth IRA very attractive as an inheritance asset.[15]

However, if you're currently worried about income, you need income, you find yourself in a higher tax bracket, or your current-year taxable income is high, it might be better to take the Roth IRA money first as part of your distribution strategy. The Roth IRA will let you access funds without having to pay more taxes, thus keeping your taxes steadier in years with big expenses and unexpected or large income.[16]

TAX BRACKETS AND SEQUENCING OF DISTRIBUTIONS

If you can save more in a Roth IRA earlier on, that's a great strategy. If you don't, when you reach age fifty-nine and a half and take a distribution from a traditional IRA or from an annuity, you'll be taxed at ordinary income tax levels, which is the highest tax rate. That means the distribution is added to your

---

15   Withdrawals of earnings prior to age 59 ½ or prior to the account being opened for five years, whichever is later, may result in a 10 percent IRS penalty tax. Limitations and restrictions may apply.

16   Guarantees are based on the claims paying ability of the issuing company.

annual taxable income, which is not good if you're in a high tax bracket.

So, which account you choose to withdraw from first depends on your overall income. Your pensions are taxed as well, but the focus should be on finding the smartest strategy based on your specific tax situation. Again, there's no cookie-cutter approach to taking withdrawals. You just want to make sure to use strategies that are tax-smart specifically for you.

As I mentioned, when someone with a traditional IRA passes away, if their spouse doesn't inherit the funds, under current tax law, a non-spouse beneficiary has ten years to distribute that entire IRA account. That's certainly something to be aware of if you have a large IRA since it could become a tax issue for your family down the road.

Conversely, a Roth IRA generally passes to heirs income-tax free. If the beneficiary is a spouse, additional options are available that can make inheriting a Roth IRA even more tax-advantageous, including the ability for the heir to treat the account as their own. Working with a certified public accountant (CPA) or a tax professional is the best way to ensure you're following the most tax-efficient strategy.

Overall, you want to take dividend income first from your non-retirement accounts and tax-free income, such as from municipal bonds. This is always a good strategy because these assets are taxed at varying levels.

ROTH CONVERSIONS AND TAXES

Roth conversions are also a strategy that can help to maximize your tax-free income in retirement. If you can convert funds from a traditional IRA to a Roth IRA during your lifetime, you will have already paid the taxes owed when you come to withdraw the funds in retirement.

Let's say you're in your fifties, and you can convert $25,000 or $50,000 a year to a Roth IRA. When you do so, you will pay taxes, and taxes are only going to go up. So, paying them now instead of later is not a bad thing. Now you've created tax-free retirement income that you will have in fifteen years' time.[17]

CAPITAL GAINS AND TAXES

Capital gains are relevant for your non-IRA accounts (brokerage accounts). Capital gains are the income you

---

17 Traditional IRA account owners have considerations to make before performing a Roth IRA conversion. These primarily include income tax consequences on the converted amount in the year of conversion, withdrawal limitations from a Roth IRA, and income limitations for future contributions to a Roth IRA. In addition, if you are required to take a required minimum distribution (RMD) in the year you convert, you must do so before converting to a Roth IRA.

earn from the sale of stock from one year to the next. You may also have capital gains or losses from the sale of other assets, such as bonds or real estate.

Long-term capital gains (gains on assets held for more than one year) are taxed at the lowest tax level, depending on someone's taxable income. That could be zero, although the average American pays about 15 percent in capital gains tax every year. If you don't have realized gains, you won't have to pay capital gains taxes.

I have clients who experience "capital gains creep." It sounds ominous, but it could be a good problem to have. Capital gains creep is when an investor is generating significant gains that they haven't realized yet. If this is the case, the investor doesn't necessarily want to pay the taxes on those gains right now.

It's advantageous to build up the gains. However, at some point the investor will have to meet their maker and pay taxes on the gains, but it will be at a lower rate than the ordinary income tax rate. The exception is for short-term capital gains (gains on assets held for less than one year), which are taxed at ordinary income tax rates.

TWO BITES OF THE APPLE

I often talk to my clients about taking two bites of the apple. In the context of building wealth for retirement, this phrase can be applied in different ways.

First and foremost, it speaks to maintaining your investment portfolio. Your portfolio will provide principal that you can draw from if you need to, and it will generate income, thus giving you two bites of the apple.

But there are other applications of the phrase. I had a client years ago who owned a pool service business. He wanted to grow his business and buy some extra routes from another company to generate more income.

We leveraged his non-retirement accounts by using a secured line of credit. He used that line of credit to buy the additional business routes. By using this method, he avoided having to take a bite out of his principal. In theory, he didn't spend any of his money to buy the new business. He maintained his investment portfolio and bought another investment by leveraging his principal. He took two bites from the apple (his principal)—and one investment paid for another.

The same can be done if you decide to invest in, for example, rental properties. You can use existing assets in your portfolio, leverage them, and buy an investment property. You maintain your existing portfolio and also gain rental income. So, again, you get two bites of the apple. You use your existing assets to get more.

Here's a specific example with dollars: Let's say you have $1 million. You're generating $50,000 a year, and you want to buy a property that will cost you $4,000 each month. You leverage your existing assets to gather a down payment for a mortgage. Now, the property you just bought is generating enough rental income to cover the $4,000 monthly mortgage payment. You own both your assets and a new income-generating property.[18]

---

18   This is a hypothetical example and is not representative of any specific situation. Your results will vary. The hypothetical rates of return used do not reflect the deduction of fees and charges inherent to investing.

PART V
GROWTH IS INEVITABLE; PROGRESS IS OPTIONAL

In the long run, it's not just about capital gains.
Dividends are the steady paychecks of investing.

—John Bogle, founder, Vanguard Group

Growth is inevitable; progress is optional. Sounds like an adage for life, not finances necessarily, but it works for both. I'll explain.

As human beings, we're pushed forward in life whether we want to be or not. As babies, we grow. We learn. Most of us aspire to progress. In the process, we also make mistakes. It's the same thing with our wealth. Most of us strive to build wealth and look for future growth opportunities in the process.

However, many don't succeed because they fail to put in the effort. They may develop bad habits like taking on credit card debt. It takes hard work, discipline, and a strategy to build wealth. In that regard, growth is inevitable, but progressive, meaningful growth is subject to your conscious effort.

What we're talking about here is commitment—commitment to a long-term saving strategy and creation of income sources. Your investments can make money for you regardless of what the market is doing. Progress is about *time in* the market, not *timing the* market.

What we're talking about here is commitment—commitment to a long-term saving strategy and creation of income sources. Your investments can make money for you regardless of what the market is doing. Progress is about *time in* the market, not *timing the* market.

If you're committed, thoughtful, and conscientious about making progress, I believe you can strive to generate income for the future. If you infuse a Reality-Based Investing mindset into your psyche, I believe you'll build a secure financial future. But to do that, you have to stay on top of your budget. You have to create income sources and diversify them.

Forget the cocktail number. Forget about the market return. Forget about what your investments have done for you in the past. It's about the progress you've made from the past to now, but it's also about the progress you're going to make in the future.

Having a financial plan is not enough. You have to be prepared to put the work in. You could have the best financial plan on paper. It could be a fifty-page glossy deck printed on the highest-quality paper. It could be premium bound. But at the end of the day, if you don't save enough money or follow the plan, the plan blows up.

Part of the reason for this is that people get distracted by the market news and the economic situation. They allow the latest headlines to dictate how they invest. Our approach is to guide our clients through the noise and keep them focused on their goals. We give them clarity so they can see how to generate the income to meet those goals.

CUTTING THROUGH THE NEWS AND NOISE

Unless you live off-grid, you most likely experience a constant 24/7 news cycle. You're bombarded with market and business news on TV, through alerts on your phone, and in emails and newsletters. It has been this way virtually since the advent of the internet. The news cycle gives us information at our fingertips, but it's also distracting and often skewed.

We now have generative artificial intelligence at our disposal too. We can use ChatGPT to set up a financial plan for ourselves. Unfortunately, that's an incredibly bad idea because ChatGPT knows nothing about you. It has no idea who you are, what your financial situation is, or how you live your life.

Watching the financial news 24/7 from the minute you wake up to the minute you lay your head back down on the pillow at night because you're worried about your portfolio is a scary and dangerous proposition. It will cause you to make bad decisions. You'll be so consumed with the amount of data coming at you that you won't be able to think straight.

This constant barrage of news can affect your financial plan, and you, detrimentally. You might watch the news and see that interest rates are rising or the stock market is tanking. But here's the thing: If you have a financial plan in place, it's all largely irrelevant.

I'll tell you something interesting. Through our broker-dealer partners and the tools that we use, we can see who among our clients accesses their online accounts and when. For example, I can see that one of our clients accessed their portfolio account three times every day last week. I can see who is most active. Why is that useful information? Because it usually tells me which clients are anxious about their portfolio—the ones who keep checking the numbers.

Ironically, when my dad was alive, he was my number one client on the anxiety scale. He was checking his account three, four, or five times a day.

"Stop checking it," I tried to tell him. "What the market is doing has no bearing on your income. You're living off the income from your portfolio, not the return on stocks, so what the market does today or tomorrow isn't going to change that."

But he was obsessed. He would access that account on his phone or his laptop from wherever he happened to be. Then, invariably, he would call me.

"Oh my God, Jay! The market's down," he'd say with a panicked voice.

He could never accept that the daily ups and downs in the market that make such compelling news are just noise. I believe, as I promised my dad, that the hype that so easily reels people in will not affect your income if your plan is a reality-based one.

Whether it's CNBC, Bloomberg, or Fox Business, whichever media outlet you tune into, they're not telling you the entire story of what's happening with your retirement income plan. They're just trying to grab your attention.

The stress that this can cause is not healthy. Giving the media your attention in this way will lead you to plan in the moment—which is a contradiction in terms.

Instead, ignore the market news. A better way to live is to determine what your goals are and plan around them. Find out what income you need and create a plan that can provide that income. Then review your plan regularly to make sure it's still working for you, because the stock market won't be.

I had a call recently from a client who had been watching the news and seeing the volatility in the markets. "Am I invested in the safest thing right now?" she asked me.

My response was no.

She freaked out.

"You're investing in diversified baskets of stock in the stock market," I told her. "The markets are volatile. But that doesn't matter because you're still generating the income you need. Your income is not volatile. It's stable."

She still wasn't convinced, so I backed up with my explanation. When President Donald Trump announced his tariffs in the spring of 2025, the market dropped 20 percent. Her portfolio did the same. However, her income remained consistent. Then the market recovered.

"You're invested in the same assets you were the month before," I told her. "Your income hasn't changed; it's just the noise within your head that has changed because you've been watching the news, the TV, and the internet."

So, don't be swayed by the hype of the day. Base your plan on your goals and your reality.

Now, over time, your life will change, and when it does, we need to talk about it. You might get a raise, buy a new house, or get married or divorced. As these changes occur, we need to decide what to do to keep your retirement plan on the right track.

Changing your plan and portfolio in response to life changes is not the same as changing your portfolio because of the market news. The review and changes I'm recommending are based on the changes going on in your life. *Your reality.* Because that's all that really matters.

When you decide to change your plan in response to life events, the reason is to maintain an appropriate level of risk. The client I mentioned who asked me whether she was invested in the safest vehicles was not necessarily risk-averse. But it's my job to assure her that her plan is maintaining the right level of risk for her reality regardless of the ups and downs of the market.

It's important to realize that anything outside of cash comes with risk. It's the degree of risk that differentiates assets and influences how you should build your portfolio.

RISK AND YOUR PORTFOLIO

Imagine you're a super risk-averse person, and you're at the beach. In this analogy, I equate being risk-averse

Ignore the market news.
A better way to live is to
determine what your goals
are and plan around them.
Find out what income you
need and create a plan that
can provide that income. Then
review your plan regularly to
make sure it's still working
for you, because the stock
market won't be.

and afraid of losing all your money with being afraid of drowning in the ocean.

If you're super risk-averse, you might worry about sharks biting you or jellyfish stinging you. In this case, you'll probably stay on the beach and not enter the water at all. I would equate this level of risk to sticking to cash and not touching other assets, like stocks or bonds.

If you're somewhere in the middle, not so scared of jellyfish and keeping an eye out for sharks, you might dip your toe into the ocean. In other words, you might dip into other investments, like municipal bonds, corporate bonds, or different degrees of fixed-income vehicles.

Now, if you're a little braver, you might wade into the water chest-deep. At this level, you risk bumping into a shark, and you could drown, but your risk is limited. In terms of the analogy, you might be investing in stocks.

So, I like to equate investing to going to the beach. If you want to be safe and not take any risk, you're staying on dry land and not venturing into the water at all. However, if you want to enjoy the bounty that the ocean has to offer, you'll have to wade in to some extent.

The risk exists because the market is volatile. Pullbacks happen. There's nothing that's a straight line about a market. Be cognizant that investing carries risk, and it's just the degree of risk that changes.

Clients often tell me, "I want to have a 20 percent return, but I don't want to take any risk."

That's awesome, but it's not reality. It's not investing in the stock market. When you set up your plan, check yourself to make sure you're comfortable with the way you decide to invest. Don't wade in chest-deep if you don't like swimming with the sharks.

You might be comfortable with the uncomfortable. Warren Buffett, the world-famous investor, said, "Be fearful when others are greedy, and greedy when others are fearful," which is much the same thing.[19]

19   Buffett, letter to the shareholders of Berkshire Hathaway Inc., February 27, 1987, https://www.berkshirehathaway.com/letters/1986.html.

Buffett takes calculated risks. He invested when a market was down to get the upside for his investors. When the market is uncomfortable for most, that's when Buffett invested. But he could afford to.

Dollar-cost averaging is another strategy that's more approachable for the retail investor.[20] As I said earlier, you can't time the market, but you can spread out your investments in the market over time so you average a return that smooths out the highs and lows. For example, you could invest five hundred dollars a month over twelve months to see a return that is an average of that period. You can smooth out the risks. Once again, it's *time in* the market, not *timing* the market.

I realize there is no Academy Award for financial advisors. Realistically speaking, we can make the best investment decisions today, but a month from now, the world could look completely different. Tariffs could be imposed, a world war could erupt, another pandemic could break out. Who could have predicted the COVID-19 pandemic and what that did to people's retirement savings? It makes planning difficult for sure.

---

20   Dollar cost averaging involves continuous investment in securities regardless of fluctuation in price levels of such securities. An investor should consider their ability to continue purchasing through fluctuating price levels. Such a plan does not assure a profit and does not protect against loss in declining markets.

The good news, however, is that planning is a positive way to make the best of what you have. It can lift your spirits if you feel confident in your financial planning.

People don't tend to dread going to see their financial advisor. Unless there are family or medical issues pressing, it's usually a good thing. You have the opportunity to review your portfolio and see the progress you've made toward your retirement or other goals. It's a time to pat yourself on the back and look forward to the future.

RETIREMENT IS NOT THE END—IT'S A NEW BEGINNING

During the 1940s–1960s, it was common to work for the same employer for decades. At the end of that time, if your employer was generous, you might have received a gold Rolex and congratulations. Then you tried to find purpose as you closed that chapter of your life.

Retirement today is very different. It's not about closing the best chapter. No two retirements are the same, but it's not the end; it's a new beginning.

What do you want the next phase of your life to look like? Do you want to have enough resources to travel? Do you want to be able to see your family and grandchildren? Do you want to volunteer and help with causes close to your heart, like children or animals in need?

People are finding increasingly creative ways to spend their retirement. But you need the resources and the funds available to support that next phase, particularly because you're likely to live a long life and be able to do more physically in retirement.

So, how much is enough?

Investment companies that advertise often flash a huge number that they claim you need for retirement. It might be several million dollars. Let's say someone tells you that you need $3 million to retire. What does that really mean?

It means nothing. That number is given with no context. What's your budget? What are your income sources?

My favorite question is when clients say to me, "I've got $1.3 million dollars saved. Is that enough for retirement?" The answer is I have no idea.

I need a lot of answers to a lot of questions before I can tell them whether $1.3 million is enough for them to retire. For example, what's their budget? What do they spend monthly? What are their income sources? Do they have an emergency budget in case they need $10,000 to replace the roof or the air conditioning or pay for a healthcare expense?

Simply coming up with a number despite having no definitive answers to those questions is not realistic. Having $1.3 million and a generic plan is not going to be enough to allow you to retire with confidence.

That's why I believe that the Reality-Based Investing philosophy works. We work with your reality and your budget. We don't develop the budget. You develop the budget based on what you spend and your lifestyle. We develop a plan based on your current assets to pursue your goals and live the next phase of your life.

THE REALITY OF RETIREMENT

You want and need to make money in retirement. If you want to have the flexibility to retire early, before you qualify for Social Security, you may have to accept that you can't access some retirement income from your IRA accounts. That means you must have enough resources to meet your retirement goals without drawing from your qualified retirement accounts.

Let's say you want to quit your nine-to-five job selling widgets. You might say to yourself, *Well, I've got enough resources to cover 70 percent of my budget.* You might decide to work part-time at Home Depot to make up the 30 percent shortfall. After all, you've done a lot of home improvement projects.

That might mean you can retire and have a part-time job that you enjoy. Alternatively, you might start an online business or offer coaching services to generate the income you need.

All of these are creative ways to ease your transition into retirement both financially and psychologically. You're not going to stop working on Friday and then sit at home eating bon-bons on Monday. Do that, and you're likely going to drive yourself nuts. That's when you might find yourself tuning in to Bloomberg, CNBC, or Fox Business and obsessively checking your funds.

The best way to ease into retirement is to have a reality-based plan. It might even spur you to do something new and fun.

PART VI

WHO IS THE RIGHT FINANCIAL ADVISOR FOR YOU?

The question isn't at what age you want to retire; it's at what income.

—George Foreman, businessman and boxer

WHAT YOU SHOULD EXPECT FROM YOUR FINANCIAL PLANNER

Knowledge and expertise are two nonnegotiables when it comes to the financial professional you work with. A third is that you have to get along with that person. You have to "gel" with them.

I often joke with people and tell them, "I'm going to know more about you than you know about yourself." More often than not, my clients come to realize that's true.

If you're going to divulge your financial and lifestyle secrets, it helps to work with someone you feel you can trust and relate to—someone you like to spend time with, even.

Financial advisors are one leg of the three-legged stool serving a client's financial needs. The other two legs are the estate lawyer, who does your estate planning, and the certified public accountant (CPA), who does your taxes.

We want each of our clients to feel like they're our only client. In short, the right financial advisor matchup

Financial advisors are one leg of the three-legged stool serving a client's financial needs. The other two legs are the estate lawyer, who does your estate planning, and the certified public accountant (CPA), who does your taxes.

is relationship-based. You have to like the person, you have to understand them, and you have to get along with them.

In my case, friends become clients, and clients become friends. It's a real relationship. The best advisors are grounded in today's reality, and they want that relationship. They also understand that what worked years ago doesn't work now. Financial planning is constantly evolving.

Many planners have shifted their approach from traditional academic financial planning to reality-based financial planning. That transition requires a shift in mindset. I understand the academic financial planning approach. I practice it to some extent, but I look at its principles through a different lens for reality-based planning.

The partnership between a client and a financial advisor is paramount. When I first work with you, I will give you an information sheet. The information laid out on that sheet is to remind you that we're dealing with your money. It's not my money. I realize you're coming to me for a service: to guide you and help you plan and select investments.

I have clients who call me and say, "Is it okay if I take five thousand from my account?"

My answer is that I don't care. I don't mean that in a flippant way. I mean it in the sense that it's your money, not mine, so I don't care how you spend it. That's your decision. But I do care that you understand the ramifications of taking that money out of your account.

If you take out five thousand dollars, I don't care what you do with it. People call me and ask permission to buy cars, houses, or boats. I'm not there to give an opinion on whether that's the right thing to spend your money on. I just want to make sure your spending fits into your overall plan.

So that begs the question, can you work with your chosen planner or advisor? Are you going to listen to them, and are they going to listen to you?

I always like to conduct an initial interview with a new client to see if we're the right fit. It might be a fifteen-minute phone call or a half-hour meeting. I recommend doing this before you decide to work with someone. Once you conclude that this is a person you can work with, you can determine whether they can do the planning and provide the services you need.

In my practice, I use a questionnaire to determine client fit. You'll find that questionnaire on my website at https://www.evervestfinancial.com/ document-center.

Your financial advisor is typically the first point of contact for anything financial, not your estate lawyer or CPA. Your financial advisor is the quarterback for your financial team. We help oversee and manage the attorneys, CPAs, and other professionals.

We are also confidantes. I sometimes receive calls about devastating events, such as a death in the family. I'm sometimes the first to be called because of the immediate financial implications. I often know tragic news before other family members. That's a heavy burden for a financial advisor to carry, but it's all part of the relationship and how it develops over time.

A relationship with a financial advisor is not a short-term endeavor. A short-term relationship is simply transactional. It's not a true planning relation-ship. Relationships with the purpose of planning will work only if they are long-term. It does the client a significant disservice from a planning standpoint if the relationship is transactional.

When you hire a financial advisor, also look at the team around them providing administrative and invest-ment support. In addition to me, my team comprises other financial advisors, administrative assistants, a client relations associate, a chief operations officer, and compliance staff. If a client wants to transfer funds, I don't complete the actual steps to make that happen.

I rely on my team to collect the administrative details and complete the transaction for that client. So, make sure that whoever you work with has an effective team that supports them while they are supporting you.

QUESTIONS TO ASK BEFORE YOU HIRE A FINANCIAL ADVISOR

I recommend asking a financial advisor certain questions before you decide to work with them. The list below might seem long, but we're talking about your money and your financial future here. You would be wise to ask as many questions as you can.

1. What's your philosophy regarding financial planning?

2. What's your philosophy regarding investing?

3. How do you invest?

4. How do you operate your practice?

5. What do you do for your clients?

6. What are your services?

7. What are your credentials?

8. Did you just get licensed, or have you been in the industry for a long time?

9. Are you a Certified Financial Planner (CFP®)?

10. What other designations do you have?

11. What continuing education do you do?

12. How long have you been in business?

13. Who's your broker-dealer?

14. Who's your custodian?

15. Are you a fiduciary, and what does that mean?

16. How are your fees structured?

The term *fiduciary* is often tossed around, but what does it really mean? There are legal requirements to being a fiduciary, specifically the requirement to operate in the client's best interests. A fiduciary is not supposed to make recommendations that would benefit themselves. But it's paramount that an advisor operates in their client's best interests regardless of whether they have the legal obligation to do so.

Fees are another critical aspect of the services your financial advisor provides. A reputable financial advisor will be transparent regarding their fee structure. Also, what are you getting for your money? Are you getting a full-blown financial plan or an abbreviated three-page plan? If the fees include an abbreviated plan, is there an additional cost for a full financial plan?

GETTING REAL, GETTING STARTED

My goal with this book has been to explain how to make retirement work for you in the real world—your world, with real expenses, real fears, real goals, and real income.

The reality of retirement today is that people are living longer. There are few, if any, pensions, and the cost of living is rising higher and higher. The cost of healthcare is on everybody's mind, and it should be.

I've prescribed a reality-based plan. It's one in which you live *off* your investments, not *on* your investments, and you're not subject to the whims of the inevitably volatile markets.

My plan will have you dissecting someone's boasting at a cocktail party and explaining that the total return equation is dividends plus market growth over time, not the market return that happened to be strong that year.

A plan takes commitment to work. It's not easy to find balance between living your life and saving. It's not easy to balance your budget and make sacrifices today so that you can reap the rewards later. I understand that, but I consider it my job to show you what you can achieve if you do those things.

This book shows you how to build a durable income pyramid. It explains the power of annuities and tax-smart withdrawal strategies. This book shows you how to leverage what you have and how to take two bites of the apple. There is a plan for you that will work.

Retirement is not different today just because we need to replace a paycheck. It's a new chapter of your life. It's a time to live again after planning for financial security.

Again, there are no silver bullets here, no methods that are one-size-fits-all—just real strategies for real people that balance income, risk, and taxes.

I hope this book has helped you to see how you can make your retirement vision a reality. Let's start by making sure the money that comes in matches what you need to go out, and the rest will follow!

https://www.evervestfinancial.com/

ABOUT THE AUTHOR

Jay R. Spector is a Certified Financial Planner™ (CFP.net) and a founding partner of EverVest Financial with his long-time friend Elizabeth Mahoney. Jay spent his early career as an assistant to former US Secretary of the Interior Bruce Babbitt in Washington, DC. He attended Johns Hopkins University, where he earned a master of science in real estate. He and his wife Bethany later moved back to his home state of Arizona, where he served as executive director of the Arizona Water Infrastructure Finance Authority in the administration of former Governor Janet Napolitano.

Jay then joined the private sector as a municipal finance investment banker. He realized that his passion was for helping friends and family with their retirement and investment planning. After some time as a vice president of municipal finance at RBC Capital Markets, Jay moved to the financial planning side of the industry, where he and Elizabeth started working together. And the rest is history.

Jay served on the City of Scottsdale's Environmental Quality Advisory Board and the US EPA's Environmental Financial Advisory Board. He serves on the board of directors for the Foster Alliance, an Arizona-based foster care resource organization as well as on the board of directors for the Ronald McDonald House of Central and Northern Arizona.

Elizabeth and Jay continue to work to fulfill their initial vision of providing families with a financial planning partnership they can trust.